HER MAJESTY QUEEN EL...
THE QUEEN MOTHER

by Rachel Stewart

Born into an aristocratic half-Scottish, half-English family, Lady Elizabeth Bowes-Lyon could not have predicted the extraordinary future that lay ahead of her. Initially reluctant to marry into royalty, she subsequently found herself, through unprecedented circumstance, a queen, helping to lead her nation through the devastating years of war. Her outstanding courage and cheerfulness were an inspiration to all and she quickly earned her people's affection.

After King George VI's death, she might easily have retired from public life. Yet a profound love of her country and a simple wish to be useful for as long as possible, prompted her to create a special role for herself as a hard-working member of the 'family firm'.

Her close attachment to her own relatives and friends, and a deep-felt concern for people who have to face difficult problems in their lives, endear her to all who meet her. Perhaps Cecil Beaton best summed up how the British feel about her when he described her as 'this great mother-figure and nanny to us all'.

ABOVE: *At home in Clarence House, Her Majesty attends to her correspondence.*
OPPOSITE: *A beautiful painting of the Duchess of York in 1925, by Philip de Laszlo.*

Public Duties

It is quite astonishing that, just three weeks short of her eighty-ninth birthday, The Queen Mother crossed the Atlantic to keep an appointment to meet the citizens of Canada. She is so concerned not to disappoint people that nothing will persuade her to give up these strenuous visits. This one involved many engagements in the sizzling heat of the Canadian summer, inspecting the Guard of Honour, visiting regiments, talking with Prime Minister Brian Mulroney, and attending formal luncheons. Yet she sailed through it all exuding a freshness and vitality that would leave many people half her age wilting from fatigue.

After her husband, King George VI, died, Queen Elizabeth had to find a new role for herself - but this was not easy. The dowager queens before her, Alexandra and Mary, widows of King Edward VII and King George V respectively, had presented somewhat remote figures, who withdrew from public life after their husbands' deaths. Queen Elizabeth

was only fifty-one when King George died and she was still full of energy, and devoted to the Royal Family and to her country. Her resolve became clear when she announced: 'My only wish now is that I may be allowed to continue the work that we sought to do together.' The problem was, how? After Elizabeth II's coronation, she tactfully decided to leave the major public appearances in Britain to her daughter, and instead to concentrate on duties abroad. She thus became an intrepid air traveller and in 1953 flew to Southern Rhodesia in a Comet. This was the first jet aircraft to land in Salisbury.

The following year she was invited back to the United States, to receive the money raised in her husband's memory to pay for the training of Commonwealth students. Her modest reaction was: 'Who is going to be interested in the middle-aged widow of a king?' At her official reception she was too nervous to eat. Yet the American public had not forgotten her and huge crowds gathered to greet her. A

newspaper described her as 'the Royal lady with the peaches-and-cream complexion and twinkling eyes', and it was the New Yorkers who first gave her that endearing nickname 'The Queen Mum'.

From then on, it was clear that she had a very important contribution to make to the work of the Royal Family and she has since made major trips abroad nearly every year, sometimes taking in several countries.

Before The Queen embarked on a visit to Australia and New Zealand in November 1953, she appointed her mother a Counsellor of State. This has involved, among other things, residing on Privy Councils, receiving ambassadors who come to present their credentials, and holding Investitures at Buckingham Palace.

While in residence at Clarence House, The Queen Mother's working day usually starts at 10 am, when she goes through the correspondence with her lady-in-waiting, either from individuals seeking advice or help, or from the hundreds of societies and charities of which she is patron or president. Then she discusses the more official mail with her private secretary, and talks about future engagements. Everything has to be planned down to the smallest detail, months, or even years, in

OPPOSITE, ABOVE: *With the children of Sark.*

OPPOSITE, BELOW: *A joyful Canadian visit.*

BELOW: *Inspecting a regiment at Sir John Moore Barracks, Winchester.*

ABOVE RIGHT: *St Mark's Square, Venice.*

BELOW RIGHT: *A favourite form of transport; alighting in Sark, 1984.*

advance. Frequently two or more appointments are crammed into one day. Shortly before her Canadian trip in 1989, The Queen Mother was in Dover in her role as Lord Warden of the Cinque Ports. She gave a reception on board the Royal Yacht *Britannia*, attended a service the following morning, visited a primary school and went on to a meeting of the Court of the Brotherhood and then celebrated her tenth anniversary as Lord Warden. The next day she was in France and two days after that in Oxford as Patron of the University of Oxford Development Programme. The latter half of June continued at the same pace, with a quick dash to Newcastle after Beating Retreat, to take in Tyne Tees Television, Hadrian's Wall and, as President of the National Trust, to open a hostel at Peel, and then back to London for a reception given by the College of Speech Therapists.

Little wonder that her Household (which she affectionately calls 'my little family') describes life with The Queen Mother as 'delightful but exhausting'.

ABOVE LEFT: *A friendly chat over the garden fence with a Sandringham neighbour. The Queen Mother always takes a special interest in people who live close to the royal homes.*

ABOVE CENTRE: *Even the pouring rain does not deter The Queen Mother from attending the Ascot Races.*

ABOVE RIGHT: *Sympathetic words from Her Majesty often provide much-needed comfort to those with disabilities. The people of Norwich greet The Queen Mother warmly at their local airport.*

LEFT: *There is always plenty to see at Trooping the Colour. The Queen Mother enjoys the company of her great-grandson, Prince William, and his mother, The Princess of Wales.*

OPPOSITE: *The Queen Mother, during a visit to RAF Marham, presents a new standard to no. 617 Squadron, who achieved fame for the 'Dambusters' raid during the Second World War.*

Favourite Grandmother

Prince Charles has said of The Queen Mother, 'Ever since I can remember, my grandmother has been the most wonderful example of fun, laughter, warmth, infinite security and, above all else, exquisite taste.' There has always been a special bond between the Prince of Wales and his grandmother. Indeed, they have much in common: a strong devotion to duty and a deep religious faith, yet a lively sense of humour and ready wit. Queen Elizabeth taught Charles to paint when he was still tiny and at the age of seven he was standing enthusiastically beside her in the river taking his first angling lessons. They are both keen organic gardeners and have a

natural belief in homoeopathic remedies.

Princess Margaret's son was christened with her mother's favourite names, David Albert Charles, and was born in Clarence House. When only two months old, he was entrusted to her loving care at Sandringham while his parents enjoyed a holiday. The eventual failure of her daughter's marriage to Antony Armstrong-Jones, of whom The Queen Mother was very fond, must have been hard to bear.

Now there are great-grandchildren to enjoy. Little Prince Henry had his first official public appearance in June 1989 at Trooping the Colour, when he rode proudly in Queen

Elizabeth's coach along with his older brother, Prince William.

Her house parties, especially at the Castle of Mey in Scotland, have been described as 'riotous', with fishing and crab-hunting, picnics and informal dinners, followed by eightsome reels. There are always plenty of young people among the guests.

The Queen Mother's vast experience of public affairs is invaluable to younger members of the Royal Family, and she is always ready to give advice. The Princess of Wales received a crash course from her in the art of being royal, shortly before her marriage to Prince Charles.

It was on her own Silver Wedding day that The Queen Mother spoke of her philosophy of family life: 'Looking back over the last twenty-five years and to my own happy childhood, I realize more and more the wonderful sense of security and happiness that comes from a loved home.'

OPPOSITE, ABOVE: Christening of Prince Henry.
OPPOSITE: An 80th birthday celebration for a much-loved mother and grandmother.
ABOVE: A hug for Prince Charles after the 1954 American tour.
RIGHT: Welcoming her eldest grandson to the Castle of Mey.
BELOW: Prince Edward listens attentively.
BELOW RIGHT: With Hackney families, London.

Lady Elizabeth Bowes-Lyon

In September 1900, Lord Glamis returned from Scotland only to discover that he had failed to register on time the birth of his ninth child, Lady Elizabeth Angela Marguerite Bowes-Lyon. He was fined seven shillings and sixpence. He even mistakenly declared that the baby had been born at their country home of St Paul's Walden Bury in Hertfordshire, whereas the event had taken place somewhere in London – perhaps even in a horse-drawn ambulance it is rumoured – no one can now remember. At least the date of 4 August is certain.

Four years later, on the death of his father, Lord Glamis became the 14th Earl of Strathmore and simultaneously inherited a vast fortune. In addition to the ancient family seat of Glamis Castle and the Hertfordshire estate, he rented a splendid Adam mansion at 20 St James's Square in London, and the family alternated between the three homes.

Elizabeth and her younger brother, David, were the two babies of the large family, and they became devoted companions, lovingly cared for by their nanny, Clara Cooper Knight, otherwise known as 'Alah'. Their favourite den at The Bury was 'The Flea House', accessible only by a very rotten ladder, where they kept a wonderful hoard of forbidden delicacies. Here they sometimes hid from their French governess, Mlle Lang, hoping to evade morning lessons.

The summer months were always spent at

Glamis Castle, which, despite its gloomy secrets (their malformed great-uncle was reputed to have been interned in a hidden room), was nevertheless filled with the sound of fun and laughter. Lady Strathmore, not only a talented musician and gardener, had, according to a friend, a 'genius for family life'.

The twelve-year-old Lady Elizabeth was devastated when David was packed off to boarding school, but at least she managed to pass her Junior Oxford Examination with some credit under the strict guidance of her new governess, Kathie Kuebler, who added German and mathematics to her existing curriculum of French, English, history, music, dancing and drawing.

On 4 August 1914, Lady Elizabeth's fourteenth birthday, war was declared and Glamis Castle was turned into a convalescent home for wounded soldiers, run by her elder sister, Lady Rose, who quickly trained as a nurse. Elizabeth spent much of her spare time assisting her, cheering up the patients, helping them to write letters and running errands for them. Then tragedy struck: their elder brother, Fergus, was killed at the Battle of Loos.

OPPOSITE, FAR LEFT: *Just seven years old.*
OPPOSITE ABOVE: *Lord and Lady Strathmore with nine of their ten children. Elizabeth is the second youngest.*
OPPOSITE: *With her 'darling Bruvver', David, her devoted playmate.*
ABOVE: *At St Paul's Walden Bury, aged nine.*
ABOVE RIGHT: *With her sister, Lady Rose.*
RIGHT: *Lady Elizabeth and Prince Albert, soon to become her husband.*

An Early Marriage

The Queen Mother has been known to say of her late husband, 'How on earth could I ever have turned him down?' But turn him down she did, not just once, but twice. It is said that Elizabeth was afraid to take on the responsibilities of marrying into royalty. Prince Albert, or 'Bertie', second son of King George V, fell in love with the radiant Lady Elizabeth one May evening in 1920 at a society ball given by Lord and Lady Farquhar at their home in Grosvenor Square. This was not the first time they had met. Fifteen years previously at a Christmas party in London, the five-year-old Lady Elizabeth had taken pity on the tongue-tied prince and fed him crystallized cherries from her cake. His childhood had not been easy. Since being made to use his right hand, although naturally left-handed, his tendency to stutter had become significantly worse. In addition, his young legs had been forced into splints to straighten them. Nevertheless,

BELOW LEFT: *The Duke and Duchess of York, on their wedding day. Elizabeth's veil was bordered with rare old lace lent by Queen Mary.*

LEFT: *A happy moment as the young couple depart for their honeymoon amidst a shower of rose petals. The crowd lining the streets was believed to number a million.*

BELOW: *Initially, the honeymoon was spent at Polesden Lacey, a fine Regency house deep in the Surrey countryside. A visit to Elizabeth's beloved Glamis followed.*

despite recurring bouts of illness, he had eventually distinguished himself as a naval officer at the Battle of Jutland during World War I. By the time Prince Albert proposed to Elizabeth, he was quickly becoming a respected figure, and George V expressed his approval by creating him Duke of York.

Permission to broadcast the couple's marriage on 26 April 1923 was refused on the grounds that 'people might hear it while sitting in public houses, with their hats on'. The bride looked dignified and composed in a medieval-style ivory wedding dress made of fine chiffon moiré embroidered with silver thread and pearls. The Duchess of York was dismayed to develop whooping cough on her honeymoon, spent partly at Glamis Castle: 'so unromantic', she wrote to her new mother-in-law, Queen Mary.

White Lodge in Richmond Park was to have been their home, but it was inconvenient and cold, so the Duchess quietly insisted that they take out a lease on a comfortable London mansion, 145 Piccadilly. Royal duties

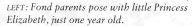

quickly crowded into Elizabeth's life: laying foundation stones, attending events, visiting hospitals, becoming president or patron of a variety of organizations and charities. Meanwhile, her husband blossomed under her loving care, and, most importantly, he was able to overcome his stammer with Elizabeth's encouragement and the help of an Australian Harley Street specialist, Lionel Logue.

In the early hours of 21 April 1926, a baby princess, named Elizabeth Alexandra Mary, was born to the Duchess of York, a happy event overshadowed in the newspapers by the gloom of the General Strike. Six months later, it was a wrench for Elizabeth to leave her baby for the royal couple's obligatory world tour. In Australia and New Zealand, the Yorks made a tremendous impression. The Governor of South Australia said of the Duchess that the whole continent was 'in love with her'.

On 21 August 1930, a second daughter was

born, this time, on the Duchess's insistence, at Glamis. She was christened Margaret Rose. And so the family was complete.

The old King was very fond of his two little granddaughters. He often used to look through his binoculars from Buckingham Palace and wave to Princess 'Lilibet' at her window in 145 Piccadilly. Shortly before his death, he said with strange foresight, 'I pray to God that my eldest son will never marry and have children, and that nothing will come between Bertie and Lilibet and the throne'. Indeed, the Prince of Wales, although popular with the public, had seriously disappointed his father, leading a self-indulgent social life that had culminated in a scandalous affair with a married American woman, Wallis Simpson.

After the death of King George V, the Yorks regarded the behaviour of the uncrowned Edward VIII with mounting apprehension. Then the King made his announcement that he was determined to marry the newly divorced Mrs Simpson. It quickly became clear that the Church of England, the Government and rulers of Commonwealth countries would not tolerate such a situation and, after long deliberations with Stanley Baldwin, the Prime Minister, Edward finally decided to abdicate in Bertie's favour on Friday 11 December 1936. 'Dickie, this is absolutely terrible,' said Bertie anxiously to his cousin, Lord Mountbatten. 'I've never even seen a State paper. I'm only a naval officer.' But Elizabeth's quiet strength supported him through those troubled times. Additionally, she somehow managed to create a warm home out of the vast and impersonal Buckingham Palace.

OPPOSITE, ABOVE LEFT TO RIGHT: *The Yorks play with their dogs at Royal Lodge. Ready to inspect Glamis Pit near Durham. War-disabled men's sale of work, 1936.*

OPPOSITE: *At Moorfields Eye Hospital, London.*

OPPOSITE, BELOW: *Middlesex Hospital, 1935.*

ABOVE: *Freedom of Edinburgh for Elizabeth, 1936.*

RIGHT: *Opening of Parliament, Canberra, 1927.*

BELOW: *The Australian tour is over.*

Queen Consort

In an attempt to re-establish confidence in the monarchy, Albert decided to be crowned as King George VI, symbolic of a return to the stability enjoyed during his father's reign. Despite nervousness, the devout religious faith of George and Elizabeth sustained them through the magnificent but lengthy coronation ceremony.

Queen Elizabeth was greatly saddened by the death of her dear mother, Lady Strathmore, in June 1938, after a long illness, and the planned State Visit to France had to be postponed. Rather than wearing the sombre colours of mourning, Queen Elizabeth decided on white, and the effect was stunning. At the suggestion of King George VI, Norman Hartnell drew his inspiration for the Queen's dresses from the graceful, dreamy paintings of Franz Xaver Winterhalter, a German artist much admired by Queen Victoria. At last Elizabeth had achieved a look that ideally suited her warm femininity - and Paris was ecstatic in its praise. Yet these were anxious times. War was beginning to look inevitable and the exiled Edward and his wife, now known as the Duke and Duchess of Windsor, were

BELOW: *Newly crowned, George VI and his Queen Consort acknowledge the crowds from Buckingham Palace balcony.*

OPPOSITE: *With President Lebrun of France, 1938. Her Norman Hartnell dresses dazzled even fashion-conscious Paris.*

OPPOSITE LEFT: *The Duke and Duchess of Windsor at their wedding, June 1937.*

OPPOSITE RIGHT: *A study of Queen Elizabeth by Cecil Beaton, Buckingham Palace, 1939.*

greatly adding to the sovereign's troubles by openly sympathising with the Nazis.

British politicians began to realize the importance of an American alliance, and here the King and Queen had a vital role to play. Braving the possible dangers of German submarines, the royal couple crossed the Atlantic in the summer of 1939 and were warmly greeted first in Canada. Queen Elizabeth's natural spontaneity delighted the crowds, especially when, after laying a foundation stone in Ottawa, she had an unscheduled chat with some Scottish stone-masons. This 'common touch', her genuine concern for ordinary people, was to set a style for royalty very different from the remote aloofness of George V and Queen Mary.

The informal and sincere friendliness of the King and Queen was extended to President Roosevelt and his wife, who had invited them to stay at their home, Hyde Park, for a relaxing weekend. They happily ate hot dogs, drank beer and swam in the Roosevelts' pool.

The newspaper coverage of their tour was adulatory. 'This has made us,' said King George VI as they arrived home to cheering crowds.

The grim years of World War II were soon upon them and the Queen's main task was to boost the morale of the British people. Altogether, the royal couple travelled more than half a million miles by train, visiting munition factories, Red Cross centres, air raid shelters, hospitals, evacuated children and military

training camps. Factory workers were so inspired by the Queen's presence that production invariably improved.

The two princesses were moved to the relative safety of Windsor, but nothing would persuade the King and Queen to leave London, despite the terrors of the Blitz. Their former home in Piccadilly was razed to the ground and then Buckingham Palace itself came under attack, when Queen Elizabeth made her famous remark, 'I'm almost glad we've been bombed. Now I can look the East End in the face.' After every raid Queen Elizabeth was among the first to face the devastation and to comfort the homeless and bereaved. One such person said, 'For him we had admiration, for her adoration.'

After the royal families of Europe began to flee from Hitler's advances and Buckingham Palace became a refuge for them, Queen Elizabeth was heard to say, 'I shan't go down like the others', as she practised her target shoot-

ing at the firing range in her garden. Despite her diminutive stature and gracious femininity, there was no doubting the steeliness of her courage. Nevertheless, she had many anxious moments during her husband's secret trips abroad to inspect the troops.

By the time VE Day eventually arrived on 8 May 1945, King George and Queen Elizabeth were exhausted. Hundreds of thousands of people thronged The Mall and cheered ecstatically as the Royal Family and Prime

Minister, Winston Churchill, waved from Buckingham Palace balcony.

War was over, but times were hard and the duties expected of the Royal Family were unrelenting. The King, as always, had to cope with the daily grind of 'the boxes', filled with important Cabinet papers for his urgent attention, and he often looked tired and strained. When Lady Airlie, an old family friend, asked him how he was coping, he replied without hesitation, '*She* helps me,' referring to his wife.

Both King George VI and Queen Elizabeth regretted the end of British rule in India, a country which they loved dearly. Their visit to South Africa, however, was happy and rewarding and the winter sunshine provided a much-needed tonic for the King's uncertain health.

The family travelled everywhere in a white and gold train, one-third of a mile long.

That summer, Princess Elizabeth's engagement was announced and on 19 November she and Prince Philip were married in Westminster Abbey. The Queen, an expert and gracious hostess, had been consulted about every aspect of its planning, who to invite, where people should sit, the style of the wedding gown and so on. It was a great comfort to the princess that 'Mummy' could be so relied on.

A few months later, on 26 April 1948, the King and Queen had a special day of their own to celebrate: their Silver Wedding. They were quite dumbfounded by the sackfuls of congratulatory letters that they received from all over the world. After the thanksgiving service in St Paul's Cathedral, they drove around twenty-two miles of London streets, waving to the enthusiastic crowds.

OPPOSITE, TOP: *Meeting Red Indians in Canada; with the Roosevelts, New York, 1939.*

OPPOSITE: *Bomb damage at Buckingham Palace, 1940.*

INSET: *The war is over! VE Day, 1945.*

TOP LEFT: *Silver Wedding, St Paul's Cathedral, 1948.*

TOP RIGHT: *Wedding day of Princess Elizabeth to Lt Philip Mountbatten, 1947.*

LEFT: *Waving farewell to Princess Elizabeth and her husband as they depart for their Commonwealth Tour, 1952.*

ABOVE: *The King and Queen with their grandchildren, Prince Charles and Princess Anne.*

Rebuilding Her Future

As 1948 progressed Queen Elizabeth became increasingly concerned about pains and numbness in her husband's legs, and finally persuaded him to consult his doctors. The diagnosis was serious: arteriosclerosis. Rest was vital, and public duties and foreign visits must be postponed. Queen Elizabeth carried on with their work alone, determined to be optimistic about the King's recovery. It was most important not to worry Princess Elizabeth, who by now was expecting her first child, due in November.

In 1951, the King was able to open the Festival of Britain, but a persistent chill turned out to be the beginning of the end. Examina-

tion revealed a malignancy in the lung, and, despite an apparently successful operation, Elizabeth was told that her husband was unlikely to live for more than eighteen months. On 6 February 1952 he died quietly in his sleep at Sandringham.

Outwardly, Elizabeth appeared to cope amazingly well. On the day of her husband's death, she played with her two grandchildren, Prince Charles and Princess Anne. 'I've got to start sometime and it is better now than later,' she said bravely. But inwardly she was bereft. Not only had she lost her husband; she had lost her life's purpose. Somehow, she would have to rebuild a very different future.

OPPOSITE, ABOVE: *Three queens mourn George VI, at his funeral, February 1952.*

OPPOSITE: *Elizabeth II is crowned in June 1953. She and her family watch the RAF flypast.*

TOP: *The remote Castle of Mey, restored by The Queen Mother.*

ABOVE: *Talking to Maori dancers, Rotorua, New Zealand, in 1966.*

RIGHT: *Important royal ambassadress for Britain, The Queen Mother visits Nairobi, Kenya.*

Her Beautiful Gardens

During the early days of her widow-hood, Queen Elizabeth went to stay with some friends in Caithness, at the northernmost tip of Scotland. It was there that she fell in love with the sixteenth-century Castle of Mey, under threat of demolition. Feeling a great wish to preserve this ancient part of Scotland's heritage, she bought the castle and restored it. Planning her new home, with its fine walled garden, helped to renew her interest in life during those desolate, lonely days of her grieving.

Each segment of the garden is sheltered from the relentless north-west wind by thick 'tapestry' hedges - a dense and fragrant mixture of shrubs and trees. Within these grows a delightful profusion of cottage flowers inter-spersed with a variety of vegetables.

Half way between Windsor Castle and Virginia Water lies the Royal Lodge, The Queen Mother's weekend retreat, a place full of treasured memories of happy times with her late husband. It was first presented to them by King George V in 1931, but at that time the garden was a wilderness. Both Bertie and Elizabeth had a real talent for landscaping and gradually, with the help of friends and relatives, they cleared the undergrowth and

ABOVE: Tranquil woodland at Royal Lodge, Windsor.
RIGHT: Wide lawns and flower beds surround Royal Lodge.
OPPOSITE: Old-fashioned flowers ramble freely within the walls of the Castle of Mey.

created delightful winding woodland walks, with lawns, paved areas and flower-beds close to the house. Today The Queen Mother particularly enjoys the scented lavender borders, the old-fashioned roses and the magnificent Lebanon cedars that spread their branches above the sweeping lawn.

The garden of Clarence House, the Queen Mother's London residence, is surprisingly large, with the plane trees providing dappled shade on warm summer days. Around the lawn are beds of vivid Pelargonium 'Sprinter', which Her Majesty can enjoy from her drawing-room windows. Early in the year, carpets of purple and white crocuses surround the handsome magnolia trees.

About eight miles from Balmoral is The Queen Mother's other Scottish retreat, Birkhall, beautifully positioned by the River Muick. This garden was also largely planned by Bertie and Elizabeth when Duke and Duchess of York, and lies, most attractively, on a slope. A particularly colourful feature is the herbaceous border which is 250 feet (76.1m) long. Late-flowering varieties predominate, to welcome Her Majesty for her visit in the early autumn.

Hobbies and Pastimes

The Castle of Mey is not only a tranquil holiday home, it is a working farm, and The Queen Mother is rightfully proud of her herd of Aberdeen Angus cattle and flock of Cheviot sheep. At heart, she is a true countrywoman and has often felt invigorated by a brisk seaside walk with her dogs, either along the rugged shores of Caithness or the sands of Norfolk, where the sharp winds 'blow away the cobwebs'.

It was Bertie's purchase of Dookie the corgi in 1933 that was the start of the royal dynasty of little Welsh cattle dogs, faithful companions of The Queen Mother and her elder daughter. Between them they currently have ten corgis and 'dorgis' (crossbred with

Princess Margaret's long-haired dachshunds). Elizabeth has a natural way with animals, having been brought up with pets in her childhood homes. Once, when visiting a bombsite during the war, she coaxed a petrified terrier out from under a heap of debris. 'I am rather good with dogs', she explained to bystanders.

The Queen Mother's love of fishing was born during those idyllic summer months at Glamis. She later shared this traditional country pursuit with her husband at Balmoral. Even in her eighties, Queen Elizabeth has donned waders to reach the best salmon, and has often been found down at the river all day. Birkhall is thus a favourite retreat for a few days during the spring.

Her great passion is for horse racing and her fine array of trophies is proof of her outstanding success as an owner. Those in the business talk of her gift of second sight; others that she knows by the expression in the horse's eyes if it will be a winner.

She owned her first horse, Monaveen, jointly with Princess Elizabeth and he won four races in the first season in 1949. In the second, the princess was broken–hearted when he fell and injured himself so badly he had to be destroyed. Thereafter she concentrated on flat racing, but her mother continued to be enthralled with racing 'over the sticks'. Peter Cazalet was the trainer of her horses, and he and his wife Zara became personal friends.

OPPOSITE, ABOVE: *The New Zealand tour in 1927 included an off-duty fishing trip.*

OPPOSITE: *Sunnyboy, The Queen Mother's 300th winner, receives a well-earned pat after coming first at the Fernbank Hurdle Race, Ascot, 1975.*

ABOVE: *With Prince Charles at the Derby.*

RIGHT: *Dancing an eightsome reel with London University students, at a ball given by the President of the Union.*

Queen Elizabeth much enjoyed her annual visits to their home near Tonbridge to watch her horses at exercise before the meeting at Lingfield. She was much distressed by Caza-let's death in 1973 and thereafter the distin-guished Fulke Walwyn took over as trainer.

By 1985, the number of her wins totalled, amazingly, more than 350. Some of her most famous horses have been M'as-tu-vu, Double Star, The Rip, Makaldar, Game Spirit, Chaou II, Inch Arran and Colonius. Devon Loch is especially remembered for his dramatic col-lapse only yards from the finishing line and a full six lengths ahead of the field in the 1956 Grand National. Overcoming her natural dis-appointment, Queen Elizabeth rushed down to comfort her jockey, Dick Francis. Her most valuable win was in 1984 when Special Cargo made a magnificent finish to take the Whit-

OPPOSITE, TOP LEFT: *Fine paintings and porcelain adorn the Saloon, Royal Lodge.*

OPPOSITE CENTRE: *Part of a set of Chelsea china collected by Her Majesty.*

OPPOSITE, TOP RIGHT: *Time off at Badminton Horse Trials, with Princess Margaret and her daughter, Lady Sarah Armstrong Jones.*

OPPOSITE BELOW: *A successful cattle breeder.*

LEFT: *One of The Queen Mother's many paintings. The artist is J.F.Herring.*

ABOVE: *The Queen Mother enjoys a brisk walk along a Norfolk beach.*

BELOW: *A treat for the royal corgis.*

bread Gold Cup, worth £25,472. Needless to say, the 'Bookies' Blower' installed at Clarence House is an essential piece of equipment.

The Queen Mother is a discerning collector of antiques and paintings, and eagerly peruses the Christie's and Sotheby's catalogues. The little rooms in the turrets of the Castle of Mey have been furnished in this manner. She particularly looks out for items that have family connections and have reappeared on the market, for example a silver ewer and dish hallmarked 1718 bearing the arms of George Bowes. Clarence House is filled with her treasures, many presented to her and others collected personally. Special display cabinets accommodate the superb array of Worcester china, Red Anchor Chelsea and other pieces of fine porcelain. Her walls are crowded with family portraits, paintings of thoroughbred horses and modern works of art, including those by Augustus John, Monet, Sickert and Lowry.

Her grand pianos remind visitors of her love of music and her many books denote an enjoyment of reading.

Like many hard-working people, there is nothing she likes better at the end of a tiring day than to put her feet up and watch a comedy show such as 'Dad's Army' or 'Yes, Minister' on television.

Honours and Patronages

In her private secretary's desk there is a special book which records and updates all The Queen Mother's patronages and presidencies, numbering more than 300. These reflect her wide range of interests, from large institutions such as the National Trust, to educational establishments like the Royal College of Music, or hospitals such as the British Home and Hospital for Incurables, and small charities and societies like the Injured Jockeys Fund and the Dachshund Club. She is most conscientious about reading all their reports and dealing promptly with correspondence.

When members of her Household tactfully suggest that perhaps she might consider discarding this or that duty, she always protests that she couldn't possibly because she enjoys it so much. One office that she has retired from, however, is the Chancellorship of London University, which, at the age of eighty, she passed on to Princess Anne. She took a lively interest in the students, and thousands have received their degrees from her at the Royal Albert Hall. In her mid-seventies she danced with the young president of the students' union at the university ball. 'How very clever of you to dance the Gay Gordons without knocking my tiara off', she exclaimed, clapping for more.

Queen Elizabeth is proud to be Colonel-in-

Chief of eighteen regiments or service units in the United Kingdom and around the Commonwealth. She is also Commandant-in-Chief of all three women's services. She considered it a very special privilege to become the first female Lord Warden of the Cinque Ports and also to be the first woman to join the parliament of an Inn as Master of the Bench of the Middle Temple.

One occasion that she finds very moving is the ancient ceremony of the Most Noble Order of the Garter at Windsor Castle every summer. Shortly after his accession, King

George VI conferred on her the exclusive honour of Lady of that order, to show the very high regard in which he held her, and to acknowledge the invaluable support she gave him as his consort.

OPPOSITE LEFT: *Attending the service of the Knights of the Garter with George VI, 1950.*

OPPOSITE: *With Prince Charles at Windsor, in their striking Garter robes.*

ABOVE: *The Queen Mother, as Colonel-in-Chief, inspects the Black Watch.*

LEFT: *In Rye, as Lord Warden of the Cinque Ports, in 1980.*

RIGHT: *As Chancellor of Dundee University, with Peter Ustinov.*

Birthday Tribute

Each year on 4 August, the crowds wait from early in the morning outside Clarence House to see their much adored 'Queen Mum' and wish her a happy birthday. She makes her appearance before lunch together with The Queen, Princess Margaret and other members of the Royal Family. Children are allowed over the barriers to present their posies of flowers, hand-made cards and poems. Queen Elizabeth is particularly enchanted with bunches of flowers tied up with scraps of wool or wrapped in kitchen foil, because she realizes that these have been cut from well-wishers' own gardens.

After chatting with the children, The Queen Mother entertains her family to lunch, in the garden if sunny, with the table and chairs elegantly set out under the spreading branches of the plane trees. Very often she rounds off the day with a visit to the theatre.

As old as the century, this remarkable lady has celebrated yet another year of devotion to duty, of love shared with her family and friends, and just the sheer fun of being alive.

**Practical
Pre-School**

Planning
for **Learning**
through

The Twelve Days
of Christmas

Rachel Sparks Linfield and Penny Coltman   Illustrated by Cathy Hughes

Contents

Published by Step Forward Publishing Limited
Coach House, Cross Road, Milverton, Leamington Spa, CV32 5PB   Tel: 01926 420046
© Step Forward Publishing Limited 2000

Planning for Learning through The Twelve Days of Christmas   ISBN: 1-902438-25-6

MAKING PLANS

WHY PLAN?

The purpose of planning is to make sure that all children enjoy a broad and balanced curriculum. All planning should be useful. Plans are working documents which you spend time preparing, but which should later repay your efforts. Try to be concise. This will help you in finding information quickly when you need it.

LONG-TERM PLANS

Preparing a long-term plan, which maps out the curriculum during a year or even two, will help you to ensure that you are providing a variety of activities and are meeting statutory requirements of the Early Learning Goals (1999).

Your long-term plan need not be detailed. Divide the time period over which you are planning into fairly equal sections, such as half terms. Choose a topic for each section. Young children benefit from making links between the new ideas they encounter so as you select each topic, think about the time of year in which you plan to do it. A topic about minibeasts will not be very successful in November!

Although each topic will address all the learning areas, some could focus on a specific area. For example, a topic on Spring would lend itself well to activities relating to knowledge and understanding of the living world. Another topic might particularly encourage the appreciation of stories. Try to make sure that you provide a variety of topics in your long-term plans.

Autumn 1	All about me
Autumn 2	Autumn
	Christmas
Spring 1	Fairy stories
Spring 2	Changes
Summer 1	Toys
Summer 2	Out and about

MEDIUM-TERM PLANS

Medium-term plans will outline the contents of a topic in a little more detail. One way to start this process is by brainstorming on a large piece of paper. Work with your team writing down all the activities you can think of which are relevant to the topic. As you do this it may become clear that some activities go well together. Think about dividing them into themes. The topic of Christmas, for example, has themes such as Advent, the Christmas story and Christmas presents.

At this stage it is helpful to make a chart. Write the theme ideas down the side of the chart and put a different area of learning at the top of each column. Now you can insert your brainstormed ideas and will quickly see where there are gaps. As you complete the chart take account of children's earlier experiences and provide opportunities for them to progress.

Refer back to the Early Learning Goals and check that you have addressed as many different aspects of it as you can. Once all your medium-term plans are complete make sure that there are no neglected areas.

Planning
for Learning
through
**The Twelve Days
of Christmas**

2   **Practical Pre-School**

Making Plans

DAY-TO-DAY PLANS

The plans you make for each day will outline aspects such as:

- resources needed;

- the way in which you might introduce activities;

- the organisation of adult help;

- size of the group;

- timing.

Identify the learning which each activity is intended to promote. Make a note of any assessments or observations which you are likely to carry out. On your plans make notes of which activities were particularly successful, or any changes you would make another time.

A FINAL NOTE

Planning should be seen as flexible. Not all groups meet every day, and not all children attend every day. Any part of the plans in this book can be used independently, stretched over a longer period or condensed to meet the needs of any group. You will almost certainly adapt the activities as children respond to them in different ways and bring their own ideas, interests and enthusiasms. Be prepared to be flexible over timing as some ideas prove more popular than others. The important thing is to ensure that the children are provided with a varied and enjoyable curriculum which meets their individual developing needs.

USING THE BOOK:

- Collect or prepare suggested resources as listed on page 21.

- Read the section which outlines links to the Early Learning Goals (pages 4 - 7) and explains the rationale for the topic of Christmas.

- This book covers a twelve-day period. It is divided into six themes, each of which presents activities for a two-day period. It is suggested that you might carry out the activities relating to Advent during the last two working days of November. This will allow the children, for example, to make a group Advent calendar. The other 'themes' would then be carried out during the final ten days of the term.

- For each theme two activities are described in detail as an example to help you in your planning and preparation. Key vocabulary, questions and learning opportunities are identified.

- The skills chart on page 23 will help you to see at a glance which aspects of children's development are being addressed as a focus each day.

- As children take part in the Christmas topic activities, their learning will progress. 'Collecting evidence' on page 22 explains how you might monitor children's achievements.

- Find out on page 20 how the topic can be brought together in a grand finale involving parents, children and friends.

- There is additional material to support the working partnership of families and children in the form of a 'Home links' page, and a photocopiable parent's page found at the back of the book.

It is important to appreciate that the ideas presented in this book will only be a part of your planning. Many activities which will be taking place as routine in your group may not be mentioned. For example, it is assumed that sand, dough, water, puzzles, floor toys and large scale apparatus are part of the ongoing pre-school experience. More and more groups are also able to offer opportunities for children to develop ICT skills. Role-play areas, stories, rhymes and singing, and group discussion times are similarly assumed to be happening as well, although they may not be a focus for described activities.

Note: Whilst Christmas is a Christian celebration, it is important that children from other cultural backgrounds enjoy and understand the activities. For these children Christmas provides a context within which activities relating to the Early Learning Goals are placed. Equally, festivals from other world religions practised by families of children within the group should be given prominence at appropriate times during the year.

USING THE EARLY LEARNING GOALS

Having decided on your topic and made your medium-term plans you can use the Early Learning Goals to highlight the key learning opportunities your activities will address. The goals are split into six areas: Personal, Social and Emotional Development, Language and Literacy, Mathematical Development, Knowledge and Understanding of the World, Physical Development and Creative Development. Do not expect each of your topics to cover every goal but your long-term plans should allow for each child to work towards all of the goals.

The following section highlights parts of the Early Learning Goals document in point form to show what children are expected to be able to do by the time they enter Year 1 in each area of learning. These points will be used throughout this book to show how activities for a topic on Christmas link to these expectations. For example, Language and Literacy point 2 is 'explore and experiment with sounds, words and texts'. Activities suggested which provide the opportunity for children to do this will have the reference L2. This will enable you to see which parts of the Early Learning Goals are covered in a given week and plan for areas to be revisited and developed.

In addition you can ensure that activities offer variety in the outcomes to be encountered. Often a similar activity may be carried out to achieve different learning outcomes. For example, during this topic children make their own Christmas cards. They will be learning about materials as they make and describe their choices of decoration, discovering aspects of technology as they fold the card and using early literacy skills as they write their messages inside.

It is important therefore that activities have clearly defined learning outcomes so that these may be emphasised during the activity and for recording purposes.

PERSONAL, SOCIAL AND EMOTIONAL DEVELOPMENT (PS)

This area of learning covers important aspects of development which affect the way children learn, behave and relate to others.

By the end of the foundation stage most children will:

PS1   continue to be interested, excited and motivated to learn

PS2   be confident to try new activities, initiate ideas and speak in a familiar group

PS3   maintain attention, concentrate and sit quietly when appropriate

PS4   have a developing awareness of their own needs, views and feelings and be sensitive to the needs, views and feelings of others

PS5   have a developing respect for their own cultures and beliefs and those of other people

PS6   respond to significant experiences, showing a range of feelings when appropriate

PS7   form good relationships with adults and peers

PS8 work as a part of a group or class, taking turns and sharing fairly; understanding that there need to be agreed values and codes of behaviour for groups of people, including adults and children, to work together harmoniously

PS9 understand what is right, what is wrong and why

PS10 dress and undress independently and manage their own personal hygiene

PS11 select and use activities and resources independently

PS12 consider the consequences of their words and actions for themselves and others

PS13 understand that people have different needs, views, cultures and beliefs which need to be treated with respect

PS14 understand that they can expect others to treat their needs, views, cultures and beliefs with respect

The topic of Christmas provides valuable opportunities for children to develop an awareness of the cultures and traditions associated with this time of year. They will be able to work as a group being sensitive to the needs and feelings of others. Many outcomes will also develop as a natural result of activities in other key areas. For example, when children play dice games within Mathematical Development they will also have the opportunity to further PS8.

LANGUAGE AND LITERACY (L)

The objectives set out in the *National literacy strategy: Framework for teaching* for the reception year are in line with these goals. By the end of the foundation stage, most children will be able to:

Children will:

L1 enjoy listening to and using spoken and written language, and readily turn to it in their play and learning

L2 explore and experiment with sounds, words and texts

L3 listen with enjoyment and respond to stories, songs and other music, rhymes and poems and make up their own stories, songs, rhymes and poems

L4 use language to imagine and recreate roles and experiences

L5 use talk to organise, sequence and clarify thinking, ideas, feelings and events

L6 sustain attentive listening, responding to what they have heard by relevant comments, questions or actions

L7 interact with others, negotiating plans and activities and taking turns in conversation

L8 extend their vocabulary, exploring the meaning and sounds of new words

L9 retell narratives in the correct sequence, drawing on the language patterns of stories

L10 speak clearly and audibly with confidence and control and show awareness of the listener, for example by their use of conventions such as greetings, 'please' and 'thank you'

L11 hear and say initial and final sounds in words and short vowel sounds within words

L12 link sounds to letters, naming and sounding the letters of the alphabet

L13 read a range of familiar and common words and simple sentences independently

L14 show an understanding of the elements of stories such as main character, sequence of events, and opening and how information can be found in non-fiction texts to answer questions about where, who, why and how

L15 know that print carries meaning and, in English, is read from left to right and top to bottom

L16 attempt writing for various purposes, using features of different forms such as lists, stories and instructions

L17 write their own names, labels and captions, and begin to form sentences, sometimes using punctuation

L18 use their phonic knowledge to write simple regular words and make phonetically plausible attempts at more complex words

L19 use a pencil and hold it effectively to form recognisable letters, most of which are correctly formed

The activities suggested for the theme of Christmas provide the opportunity for children to respond to stories and to participate in role play. The writing of name labels for party bags and filling stockings with words or pictures will help children to develop their early writing skills. Writing and investigating the greetings in Christmas cards will help children to know that words carry meaning and therefore give

purpose
to their own writing.
Throughout all the activities
children will be encouraged to communicate
fluently with meaning.

MATHEMATICAL DEVELOPMENT (M)

These goals cover important aspects of mathematical understanding and provide the foundation for numeracy. They focus on achievement through practical activities and on using and understanding language in the development of simple mathematical ideas.

The key objectives in the *National numeracy strategy: Framework for teaching* for the reception year are in line with these goals. By the end of the foundation stage, most children will be able to:

M1   say and use number names in order in familiar contexts

M2   count reliably up to ten everyday objects

M3   recognise numerals 1 to 9

M4   use language such as 'more' or 'less', 'greater' or 'smaller', 'heavier' or 'lighter' to compare two numbers or quantities

M5   in practical activities and discussion begin to use the vocabulary involved in adding and subtracting

M6   find one more or one less than a number from one to ten

M7   begin to relate addition to combining two groups of objects and subtraction to 'taking away'

M8   talk about, recognise and recreate simple patterns

M9   use language such as 'circle' or 'bigger' to describe the shape and size of solids and flat shapes

M10   use everyday words to describe position

M11   use developing mathematical ideas and methods to solve practical problems

During the activities suggested in this Christmas work, children will explore several aspects of shape and pattern. Sorting, matching and making Christmas cards and making tree decorations give experience of 2D shapes, and investigating and describing parcels extends familiarity with shapes that have three dimensions. Printing wrapping paper and making paper chains are used to give experience of copying, continuing and making repeating patterns. Counting is a continuing theme throughout as children develop confidence in number names and order.

KNOWLEDGE AND UNDERSTANDING OF THE WORLD (K)

By the end of the foundation stage, most children will be able to:

K1   investigate objects and materials by using all of their senses as appropriate

K2   find out about and identify some features of living things, objects and events they observe

K3   look closely at similarities, differences, patterns and change

K4   ask questions about why things happen and how things work

K5   build and construct with a wide range of objects, selecting appropriate resources and adapting their work where necessary

K6   select tools and techniques they need to shape, assemble and join the materials they are using

K7   find out about and identify the uses of everyday technology and use information and communication technology and programmable toys to support their learning

K8   find out about past and present events in their own lives, and in those of their families and other people they know

K9   observe, find out about and identify features in the place they live and the natural world

K10 begin to know about their own cultures and beliefs and those of other people

K11 find out about their environment and talk about those features they like and dislike

The topic of Christmas provides an opportunity to help children experience goals K1 to K9. In particular, as they work to produce decorations, cards and presents, they will be able to explore materials and to enjoy cutting, folding and gluing. Within all their work children should be encouraged to talk about their observations and to consider similarities, differences, pattern and change.

PHYSICAL DEVELOPMENT (PD)

By the end of the foundation stage most children will be able to:

PD1 move with confidence, imagination and in safety

PD2 move with control and co-ordination

PD3 show awareness of space, of themselves and of others

PD4 recognise the importance of keeping healthy and those things which contribute to this

PD5 recognise the changes that happen to their bodies when they are active

PD6 use a range of small and large equipment

PD7 travel around, under, over and through balancing and climbing equipment

PD8 handle tools, objects, construction and malleable materials safely and with increasing control

Activities such as the cracker game and the shepherd and wolves game will encourage children to move with co-ordination, imagination and control. Through working as a whole group children will become aware of the restrictions of space and the needs of others. Games such as tree skittles and aiming bean bags into Christmas boxes will encourage children to use small apparatus with increasing skill.

CREATIVE DEVELOPMENT (C)

By the end of the foundation stage, most children will be able to:

C1 explore colour, texture, shape, form and space in two and three dimensions

C2 recognise and explore how sounds can be changed, sing simple songs from memory, recognise repeated sounds and sound patterns and match movements to music

C3 respond in a variety of ways to what they see, hear, smell, touch and feel

C4 use their imagination in art and design, music, dance, imaginative and role play and stories

C5 express and communicate their ideas, thoughts and feelings by using a widening range of materials, suitable tools, imaginative and role play, movement, designing and making, and a variety of songs and musical instruments

During this topic children will experience working with a variety of materials as they make collage presents, decorations and cards. Through using decorations, Christmas stamps and old Christmas cards they will be able to explore colour and respond to what they see, touch and feel. The use of finger puppets to enact the Christmas story will allow children to use their imaginations, to listen and to observe. Stories throughout the topic provide a key stimulus for listening, looking and responding.

DAYS 1 AND 2

ADVENT

You need to plan to make the Advent calendar at the end of November so that the first door can be opened on 1st December

PERSONAL, SOCIAL AND EMOTIONAL DEVELOPMENT

- Discuss Advent as the time approaches Christmas. Talk about how children prepare for Christmas with their families. Explain that some people do not celebrate Christmas and that some celebrate different festivals. Draw on children from the group who can talk about festivals from other world religions. (PS4, 5)

LANGUAGE AND LITERACY

- On a large sheet of paper draw a Christmas tree. Explain that over the next two weeks the group is going to make a collection of Christmas words. On bauble shaped pieces of paper scribe for the children words they suggest to do with Christmas and stick them on the tree. (L8)

- Make a Santa's workshop role-play area. (L1, 4)

MATHEMATICAL DEVELOPMENT

- Look at Advent candles. Count the rings. From paper make a large candle for the number of days until the holidays. Each day cut off one segment and count how many remain. (M1, 2, 5)

- Play a simple dice game in which counters are moved along a candle-shaped number track to reach the flame. Encourage children to recognise the number on the die and to count out loud as they move their counter. (M1, 2)

KNOWLEDGE AND UNDERSTANDING OF THE WORLD

- Make Christmas wreath decorations. Prepare bases by cutting the centres from large card circles. Supply leaves and small fir cones to decorate. Discuss the materials as the children use them to decorate their wreaths. Supply red ribbon bows to add the finishing touch. (K2, 5,)

PHYSICAL DEVELOPMENT

- Play a counting movement game in which children do one jump, two hops, three strides, four .... Depending upon children's knowledge of numbers the game can be played up to 24. Invite children to make suggestions for the movements. (PD1, 2)

CREATIVE DEVELOPMENT

- Make a large group Advent calendar which might involve several notice boards. The calendar should include items which can be removed each day (stars, snowballs) and could contain small surprises for the children (for example chocolate pennies, stickers). Effective calendars are:

  A snow scene where each child makes a snowman or person for the calendar. The doors are white circles - snowballs. The scene could be based on a *Where's Wally?* type picture in which all the people are dressed in clothes of similar colours. Each day, as well as looking for the 'door', children could be encouraged to spot Wally who should be moved before the children arrive and who does not always need to be on the calendar! (C1)

  A scene depicting a shiny red post-box, envelopes and Christmas stamps. (C1)

  A traditional Bethlehem manger scene. This could either be silhouettes from black paper, which includes stars made by the children, or a 3D manger in which children make the characters from plastic bottles, fabrics, wool or paper and stand them in front of a star frieze. (C1)

ACTIVITY: Post-box Advent calendar

Learning opportunity: Exploring the colours and pictures on postage stamps. Making stamps for the group Advent calendar.

Early Learning Goal: Creative Development. Children will explore colour in two dimensions.

Resources: A collection of envelopes numbered from

1 to 24; paper cut into stamp shapes with pinking shears; crayons, felt pens and pencils; glue; a cut-out of a large, shiny, red post-box mounted on a wintry display scene; examples of Christmas edition stamps (postcards of stamps are ideal as they can be viewed by the whole group at once); an example of an Advent calendar.

Organisation: Whole group.

Key vocabulary: Days, weeks, months.

WHAT TO DO:

Show the group an Advent calendar. Talk about what it is used for. Explain that the group is going to make an Advent calendar. Show the children the post-box display and the envelopes. Explain how the envelopes are numbered, and that one is going to be opened each day until Christmas.

Invite the children to make Christmas stamps to go on the envelopes. What makes a stamp eye catching? What colours are 'Christmassy'? Show children examples of real stamps.

Give each child a stamp shaped piece of paper to decorate. Encourage children to do several and to pick their favourite for the calendar. (Spare stamps can be kept for envelopes for cards children make before the end of the term.) After the children have gone home you can place a surprise in each envelope.

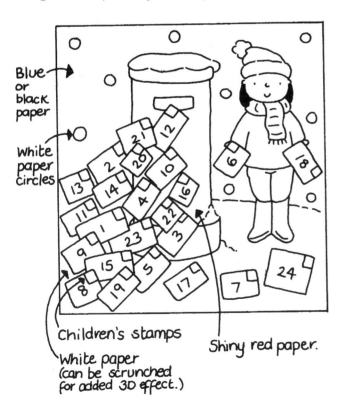

Blue or black paper

White paper circles

Children's stamps

White paper (can be scrunched for added 3D effect.)

Shiny red paper.

The envelopes can then be stapled across one corner onto and cascading from the post-box.

ACTIVITY: Santa's workshop role-play area   L+L .

Learning opportunity: Developing and discussing imaginative ideas as children work together in constructing a role-play area.

Early Learning Goal: Language and Literacy. Children will use language to imagine and recreate roles.

Resources: Two tables; safe scissors; glue or sticky tape; a collection of glittery papers; boxes; recycled materials; decorative materials; note pads and pencils; a world map; toy or Christmas shopping catalogues.

Organisation: Involve as many children as possible in assembling the area, a few at a time.

WHAT TO DO:

Explain to the children that together they are going to make a Christmas workshop. They will be able to pretend to be Father Christmas and his helpers. They have so many toys to make for delivery - the weeks before Christmas will be quite hectic!

Involve the children in equipping a workbench with tools and resources for making things. Encourage the children to offer ideas. What would Santa need?

Talk about how children write to Santa with their Christmas requests. Invite the 'writing' of order forms by adding notepads, pencils and a couple of covered shoe boxes labelled 'In tray' and 'Work done'.

Finishing touches might include a route map on the wall, pictures of reindeer, toy catalogues to act as sources of inspiration (for making and writing), a delivery sack and one or two elfin hats.

DISPLAY

Mount the tree made in the first Language and Literacy activity at floor level near the role-play area. Encourage children to add decorations to the tree over the coming days. On a table start a display of favourite Christmas picture books.

DAYS 3 AND 4

CHRISTMAS DECORATIONS

PERSONAL, SOCIAL AND EMOTIONAL DEVELOPMENT

- Use the story of 'The Smallest Tree' (in which it is the smallest tree which is chosen to be a Christmas tree) to discuss the importance of treating others with sensitivity and appreciating that everyone has special qualities to contribute. (PS2, 4)

LANGUAGE AND LITERACY

- Discuss the party which will be held on the last day of term. Decorate letters to parents requesting food for the party. (L16)

- Make name labels to be attached to individual party bags for each child at the party. (L16)

- Read *The Little Christ Child and the Spiders* by Jan Peters (Macdonald), in which tinsel is likened to a spider's web, or a tale of how Christmas trees came to be. (L3)

MATHEMATICAL DEVELOPMENT

- Encourage children to sort paper shapes into circles, triangles and squares. Use the shapes to make decorations to hang on the tree started in the Advent sessions. (M9)

- Make paper chains using strips of sticky paper which are based upon repeating patterns such as red, yellow, green, red, yellow, green. Some of the chains can be used to decorate the room and also the role play area. (M8)

KNOWLEDGE AND UNDERSTANDING OF THE WORLD

- Ask children to help Santa to sort a range of materials for use in making decorations - see activity right. (K1, 3)

- Talk about the Christmas decorations which children have seen in supermarkets, shopping centres, or perhaps street lights. Encourage the children to express ideas and preferences, and to compare different displays they have seen. (K11)

PHYSICAL DEVELOPMENT

- Play the cracker game (see activity opposite). (PD1, 2, 3)

- Make and use Christmas tree skittles from plastic bottles and crepe paper. (PD6)

CREATIVE DEVELOPMENT

- Unpack a box of favourite decorations (a shiny bauble, wooden angel, small bear). Discuss with children what makes the decorations special. Encourage children to choose one and to make up a story about it. (C3, 4)

- Make stars from card and shiny materials to hang from the ceiling. (C1)

ACTIVITY: Sorting materials for Father Christmas

KUW.

Learning opportunity: Sorting materials according to properties such as shiny, paper, fabric.

Early Learning Goal: Knowledge and Understanding of the World. Children will look closely at similarities and differences.

Resources: a mixed collection of scraps of shiny materials, fabrics, papers; glue; scissors; A4 card cut out into tree, star and stocking shapes; letter from Father Christmas.

Organisation: Whole group introduction, up to six children on the practical activity.

Key vocabulary: Shiny, dull, smooth, rough.